FINDING BEAUTIFUL

HOW THE SEARCH FOR BEAUTY LEADS US INTO THE WONDER OF GOD

FINDING BEAUTIFUL

HOW THE SEARCH FOR BEAUTY LEADS US INTO THE WONDER OF GOD

Matthew S. Miller

Renewed Christian Living
TULLAHOMA, TN

Copyright © 2017 by Matthew S. Miller.

All rights reserved. No part of this publication may be reproduced, distributed or transmitted in any form or by any means, including photocopying, recording, or other electronic or mechanical methods, without the prior written permission of the publisher, except in the case of brief quotations embodied in critical reviews and certain other noncommercial uses permitted by copyright law. For permission requests, write to the publisher, addressed "Attention: Permissions Coordinator," at the email address below.

Matthew S. Miller/Renewed Christian Living
renewedchristianliving@gmail.com
www.renewedchristianliving.com

Publisher's Note: All Scripture quotations unless otherwise listed are from The ESV® Bible (The Holy Bible, English Standard Version®), copyright © 2001 by Crossway, a publishing ministry of Good News Publishers. Used by permission. All rights reserved.

Book Layout ©2017 BookDesignTemplates.com

Ordering Information:
Quantity sales. Special discounts are available on quantity purchases by corporations, associations, and others. For details, contact the "Special Sales Department" at the address above.

Finding Beautiful: How the Search for Beauty Leads Us into the Wonder of God/ Matthew S. Miller. -- 1st ed.
ISBN-13:
978-1981689156
ISBN-10:
198168915X

*To Sailor, Macy, and Reilynn
You show me every day the wonder, truth, and beauty of
God. You three are my joy and I love you deeply.*

Contents

000 Why Beauty?.. 1
001 What Is Beauty?... 9
002 Beauty Is Spiritual... 15
003 The Beauty of All Things................................ 21
004 A Broken Beauty... 27
005 Beauty Is with Us.. 35
006 The Beautiful Savior....................................... 43
007 The Beautiful Church..................................... 53
008 Finding Beautiful.. 63

Acknowledgements

This is probably one of the most difficult parts of writing a book. Trying to give recognition to the people and influences who have shaped your journey is an impossible task, for no book could hold all the pages. However, there are those you realize directly impacted the work, the effort, and the construction, and I would be amiss if I did not give them the credit they so richly deserve. First, I must give all glory to God, the originator of life, the author of beauty, and the Father who tenderly leads me through His grace, of which I am least worthy.

I also am grateful for the constant love and encouragement from my family. My wife, Linsey, the one who is my beautiful joy and who cheered me during the multiple readings of the manuscript. My children, who show me the gift of beautiful love and celebration every day. My parents and brother, who show me the beauty of a life lived with perseverance, integrity, and family bonds.

I am also indebted to the congregations of Yadkinville church of Christ and Highland Hills church of Christ, both who allowed me the original space to begin exploring these ideas in lessons and sermons. The gift of freedom to think and explore God is wonderful, and these two families have shown me how beautiful church can be.

I want to thank my beta readers, especially Fran Lawson, Kasey Guinther, and Beanie Taylor. They are a fantastic group and were tremendously helpful in working on this book.

I also want to thank Hayley Cruz for her wonderful editing. I always look forward to working together to bring out the best of the book.

There are many others not listed that deserve commendation, and I thank God for each one and their influence in my life.

And finally, I thank you, my readers, for your constant inspiration and investment into my work. I pray that this book blesses you with a deeper awareness of the wonder of beauty in your journey of faith.

Lead us, O God, from the sight of the lovely things of the world to the thought of thee their Creator; and grant that delighting in the beautiful things of thy creation we may delight in thee, the first author of beauty and the Sovereign Lord of all thy works, blessed for evermore.

–GEORGE APPLETON

000 Why Beauty?

CHAPTER 000

Why Beauty?

Have you ever been on the verge of something new? Perhaps it was an idea you had that if it were just put into production, it would make a great product or service. Or maybe it was a new opportunity, one that if you didn't walk through, you would be missing an important step in your life. Or perhaps it is a relationship that if you hadn't stopped to pick up that coin for her, you would have never met or married or had children.

I have been in search of something for some time now, something that could change how we see one another, the world, and maybe even the nature of life itself! Okay, maybe that sounds a little too epic . . .

But it is one of those searches that I feel deep in my bones—like if I fail to embark on this, we might just miss something God intends to be meaningful and profound and transformative. And while I sense that this is a great mission set before me, I don't believe it is one to be completed alone. On the contrary, this must be a shared journey. Therefore, here I am with you, endeavoring to do something new, something that will stir us to be lost in wonder and awe. So, you are probably wondering at this point, "What in the world are you leading us into?"

Well, my friends, I am on a search to find the beautiful.

Wait a second, you may be thinking . . . *finding the* beautiful?

Overcoming fear is life changing; getting a new career, a degree, skydiving, a blind date (for better or worse) is life changing, but beauty . . . really?

When you sit back and think of all the ways we use that word, it doesn't really seem to equate to something that is, you know, "life changing." We use that word to describe a product, an industry, or a certain look that we find pleasing.

Isn't beauty just a subjective value that we place on things we appreciate? That seems plausible, right? But what if our ideas of what is beautiful and what isn't have less to do with the authentic nature of beauty and more in line with our cultural norms?

While we may all agree that musical compositions, expressive dance, or natural landscapes and artwork contain something of the beautiful, the common usage of beauty in Western society is an entirely different notion.

Think about how true this assessment is. You waltz into your local superstore and immediately notice giant photos of flawless people eating perfectly symmetrical fruit. As you proceed around the store, you pass the eyewear, swimwear, clothing, and "beauty" sections, all with people modeling products with the "perfect body" (whatever that means). After having been bombarded with these images at almost every point in the store, you stand in the checkout line where, lo and behold, the racks are filled with magazines of, you guessed it, images of "perfect people."

These daily meccas to the temples of a consumer culture provide the perfect environment to evangelize our greatest value.

You see, beauty (as communicated in such environs) demonstrates that the word as commonly used in our day has been hijacked by a "me" culture. During its captivity, it has been employed to coerce, manipulate, and downright bully people into buying a certain product or having a specific body type (often at extreme and dangerous measures), all in hopes of becoming "beautiful."

Is this the epitome of beauty? Is this where it is found?

In our search to finding the beautiful, have we reached the peak of its truth? It's like, sorry to disappoint you, being that you bought this whole book, but finding the beautiful can be found in this introduction.

It requires a slim figure, the fanciest clothes, and the most expensive makeup. If you have none of these things, take extreme financial and surgical measures, whatever it takes to get them.

If this is the case, then the rest of this book is just empty pages. You can set it down now and continue life as normal.

Your journey is completed . . . (If you set the book down, please, it's time to pick it back up!)

This understanding of "beauty" isn't very beautiful, is it?

It all just seems so artificial, so superficial. It's like watching someone perform a card trick. All along, they're telling you that it is real, that they really spit out the card that you just placed in the deck (or whatever crazy card tricks are current now), all while you know it's just smoke and mirrors. It isn't real.

Sure, it may grab our attention and may even seem real. But it isn't.

But how do we know?

When I was in college, there was a performance hall that hosted various musicians throughout the year. One performance I was especially excited about was a world-renowned violin player. So, Linsey (my fiancée at the time but now my lovely bride) and I went to go hear him and others who were performing with him.

As we sat there listening, tears began to stream down my cheeks. It was like something burst inside me, and I couldn't hold them back. The people around us were probably thinking, "What is up with that guy?"

But there was something indescribable happening, and the only way I could express it was through tears.

There have been numerous events in my life, such as celebrating when my mom, dad, and brother graduated from their schools, my baptism, watching sunsets and sunrises, peering over the coast or the mountains for the first time, staring my soon-to-be wife in the eyes as we recited our vows, holding my newborn children, being released from struggles and finding freedom, and the small everyday occurrences too numerable to list, that can only be described with one word:

Beautiful.

I am sure you can say the same. There have been occasions in your life where you catch sight of the awe of the moment and think, "How beautiful."

In our journey, we have these brushes with something that draws us beyond ourselves, beyond the shallowness of culture and into something other, something deeper.

As we begin our endeavor together, I am realizing that the nature of this kind of beauty isn't pedestrian, it's transcendent.

Maybe the whole reason we have this concept so twisted around is that we either have assumed too much about the sufficiency of culture's definition (aka, it's when something looks real pretty) or we have been looking in the wrong places.

Whatever we might say beauty is, the first step of our search is to realize that when we start looking in the right place, we may find that beauty is beyond anything we have realized before. So, where do we look for the truth of beauty?

That is what the rest of this book is about. It is about experiencing something authentic, good, and truthful. It is about finding real beauty, its purpose, and its role in our journey of faith.

The following pages are meditations, thoughts that I've had and things I've discovered in my own search for finding the beautiful.

I do not present them as the final word or even as satisfactorily approaching the search. I realize my own limitations.

However.

I pray that as you work through the meditations, something awakens in you . . . an awareness of the beautiful that has been all around us the whole time. I pray that, though I am imperfect in my own knowledge, God would somehow take me, this flawed earthy vessel, and utilize this book to let me join you in your journey to finding the beautiful.

And so, I offer this book as a gift for the life of the church, in hopes that it will help us all gain a profound awareness of the mystery and spirit of this wonder we call beauty.

Godspeed on your journey!

Soli Deo Gloria!

Your Brother in Christ,

Matthew S. Miller

Thanksgiving 2017

001 What Is Beauty?

CHAPTER 001

What Is Beauty?

What is beauty? Is beauty subjective, an object that varies by society or social makeup, held in the eye of the beholder?

Or is beauty a product, something we can put on or take off?

Perhaps beauty is an industry, just one more part of a consumer culture.

Is beauty personal and physical, consisting of how youthful we appear or what size jeans we wear?

Or maybe it's about looking like the manipulated images of models on magazine covers?

Western culture's narrative on beauty has defined it primarily in utilitarian terms, employing beauty to manipulate, coerce, deceive, and even oppress to serve the desires of those defining "beauty."

This kind of "beauty" has trickled into the heart of society, encouraging everything from bullying, body-shaming, and extreme surgical measures used to modify one's looks so a person may be found "culturally acceptable." Margaret Feinberg in the book, *The Organic God,* writes:

> Our modern culture has watered down beauty to mean little more than prettiness, popularity, or likeability. We speak of the "beautiful people" as those who possess something we do not, and we cheapen beauty to a list who who's hot and who's not.
>
> Beauty is used to describe anything and everything we prefer. We're even taught to select our produce by that which looks best—namely, large and shiny—and as a result, we often pass by the organic selection. We prefer fruits and vegetables that are attractive on the outside but affected by pesticides and chemicals on the inside.[1]

What if deep in the psyche, beauty is an experience that transcends boundaries and speaks to the core of what it means to be human?

Maybe, just maybe . . .

Beauty is fundamentally more.

What if beauty—authentic beauty—has nothing to do with an industry, a cosmetic, or age?

---

[1] Margaret Feinberg, *The Organic God* (Grand Rapids: Zondervan, 2007, 50.

It knows nothing of coercion, force, or oppression.

Authentic beauty elevates and unites us at a deeper level.

Because at its fundamental . . .

Beauty is spiritual.

/ 002 Beauty Is Spiritual

CHAPTER 002

Beauty Is Spiritual

Because beauty is profoundly spiritual, we must look beyond our ordinary usage of the term for its meaning.

When we do, we see that spiritual beauty is distinct from the value of what is commonly called beautiful because in it, we find its source.

As Paul Tripp explains:

> In this world, there is source beauty and reflected beauty. Source beauty is true beauty, pure beauty timeless beauty, independent beauty, definitional beauty, divine beauty. [2]

It is source beauty that is truly authentic . . . unassumingly transcendent.

---

[2] Paul Tripp, "Psalm 27: The Theology of Beauty," Christianity.com, August 29, 2012, http://m.christianity.com/blogs/paul-tripp/psalm-27-the-theology-of-beauty.html.

This beauty is evocative.

Therefore, the psalmist writes:

> One thing have I asked of the LORD, that will I seek after: that I may dwell in the house of the LORD all the days of my life, to gaze upon the beauty of the LORD and to meditate in his temple.[3]

Of the infinite aspects of God's identity, there are three characteristics where we identify His beauty most clearly. These three features are His glory, His community, and His love, and each of these connect us to beauty's source.

God's glory often shows up in Scripture in His temple, the place where people connect with God. And it is this glory that is associated with His beauty. As one author has said:

> If we admire the glory of God, we are admiring God's beauty. If the glory of God has an effect in our lives, God's beauty is having an effect. If God acts to magnify this glory, he is acting to magnify his beauty.[4]

Beyond His glory, God's community is steeped in mystery.

Christians for centuries searched for a way to communicate the truth of God's community, the fact that God is three in one and

---

[3] Ps. 27:4 ESV
[4] John Piper, "How Pervasive and Practical is the Beauty of God?," Desiring God, July 7, 2013, www.desiringgod.org/articles/how-pervasive-and-practical-is-the-beauty-of-god.

one in three and came to the recognition that God's triune nature is deeply puzzling.

These ancient Christians described this mystery with the Greek word *perichoresis*, a mutual interchange of movement. Another way to think of it is as a dance.[5]

Think about dancing for a moment.

Dance is an art filled with grace, emotion, and movement. It is responsive, reacting to the contours of the partner's steps in this joyous give-and-take exchange.

And dance is beautiful.

God, in His infinite Community, is engaged in this mysterious dance of grace and redemption and creating and movement, mutually responding to Himself in this joyous exchange.

And it is beautiful.

That is why God shares it.

Edmund Rybarczyk writes in his book, *For Him Who Has Eyes to See: Beauty in the History of Theology,* that:

> God is the archetype of beauty and the essence of beauty, but God didn't cling to that beauty as His sole

---

[5]Literally, this is translated as interpenetration or circumincession. While there are some differences between the Greek word for dance and the word for interpenetration, dance is an apt description of this mutual Community of Being of God's nature.

possession, something to be guarded. God unselfishly shared that because it is God's nature to love.[6]

Central to mystery of faith is this:

Beauty finds its source in our triune God, and it is this beauty that flows from His love and fills all things.

His beauty fills all things.

---

[6] Edmund J. Rybarczyk, *For Him Who Has Eyes to See: Beauty in the History of Theology* (Eugene, Ore.: Cascade, 2016), 28.

003 The Beauty of All Things

CHAPTER 003

The Beauty of All Things

In the beginning, God created the heavens and the earth. The earth was wild and waste, and darkness was over the face of the waters.[7]

And God said, "Let there be light," and there was light. And God saw that the light was . . .

Good.

God created all things and then declared it . . .

Good.

Butterflies . . . Good.

Fish . . . Good.

Trees . . . Good.

---

[7] From Gen. 1.

Cultures and cities and the flourishing of humanity . . . Good.

This word for good in the Greek translation of the First Testament[8] means more than just acceptable or satisfactory.

The Greek word *kalos* also means . . .

Beautiful.

Creation was beautiful.

But why? What is it that makes creation beautiful?

Creation is beautiful because it is a reflection of its source, of the One whom Augustine called:

The Beauty of all things beautiful.

And it is abundant, fruitful, and endlessly creative.

It is full of potential and life and order.

Ancient church writer Basil of Caesarea demonstrates this by writing, "The world is a work of art set before all for contemplation, so that through it the wisdom of Him who created it should be known."[9]

---

[8] The First Testament is the designation given throughout the rest of this book for the "Old Testament." The Greek translation of the First Testament is called the Septuagint.
[9] Qtd. in Ruth Bancewicz, "Beauty, Science, and Theology, Part 3," BioLogos, July 25, 2012, http://biologos.org/blogs/archive/beauty-science-and-theology-part-3.

This creation makes us aware of God's presence.

As Paul so boldly states in Romans 1.20:

> For His invisible attributes, namely, His eternal power and divine nature, have been clearly perceived, ever since the creation of the world, in the things that have been made. So, they are without excuse.

To put it another way, beauty in creation is our connecting point with God.

As it says elsewhere in the Psalms:

> The heavens declare the glory of God, and the expanse proclaims His handiwork.[10]

Could it be that recognition of beauty in creation is not only a human trait but also something that the creation itself is aware of and proclaiming?[11]

An interesting thought.

---

[10] Ps. 19:1

[11] A study published in the journal *Behavioural Processes* in October 2013, Vol. 99:26-33 demonstrates that fish may demonstrate preferences of music, and it has long been recognized (even Darwin himself made this observation) that animals are attracted to various attributes that we would describe as beautiful. See "Why Have Animals Evolved a Sense of Beauty?" (www.bbc.com/earth/story/20150511-why-are-animals-so-beautiful).

On any account, in this Genesis creation account, God is taking His creation from "wild and waste" to an ordered creation.

Ancient church writer St. Thomas Aquinas once wrote, "Each creature manifests God in some way, but the best manifestation of God is the beautifully ordered universe of all creatures functioning in relation to one another as God intended."[12]

It is this ordering of creation that brings things to be, therefore even being itself is . . .

Beautiful.

Therefore, creation, in its very existence, its own "beingness,"[13] demonstrates these qualities that Aquinas calls integrity, harmony, and clarity.

Like a stunning oil painting of a landscape or a photo of your children playing, these aspects reflect in some mysterious way the truthful beauty of our triune God.

But lamentably, those responsible for tending to this beautiful world would come to usher something other than beauty into it.

Instead, they brought a broken image.

---

[12] From Bancewicz, "Beauty, Science, and Theology, Part 3."
[13] I'm not quite sure this is a word, but it works!

004 A Broken Beauty

CHAPTER 004

A Broken Beauty

Looking into the mirror of the created order, creation was a complete reflection, proportional, living in harmony, and demonstrating His glory brilliantly.

But after the Fall, the mirror was broken. Our reflected beauty now brought pain.

As Tripp writes: "Reflected beauty is [now] shadow beauty, tainted beauty, dependent beauty, ill-defined beauty, creation beauty."[14]

When we sin, we sin "against beauty." He continues:

> Idolatry puts reflected beauty in source beauty's place. Sin hammers reflected beauty in the shape of ugly. Sin then names ugly beautiful. The more distant it is from its source the less beauty there is to be found in reflected beauty.[15]

---

[14] Tripp, "Psalm 27: The Theology of Beauty."
[15] Ibid.

There was a break in the order. The image is unclear.

We are now looking into a mirror dimly.[16]

John Navone writes in his book, *Toward a Theology of Beauty*, that:

> In contrast to true beauty, the allure of all that attracts us to our ultimate happiness and fulfillment, *seductive* beauty is the allure of all that entices us to our ultimate unhappiness and destruction.[17]

We have lost something of the original beautiful nature because in our desire for the tainted and seductive beauty, we left Eden, that temple in which we walked openly with God's glory. As a result, where there was once harmonious order . . . now disorder has been ushered in.

Where there was the beauty of presence, now there is profaned absence.

We are east of Eden, exiles in a world that toils to take this stuff of the earth and reflect divine beauty.

We are displaced wanderers, longing for our roots, with our collective memory of Eden growing hazier by the day.

---

[16] See 1 Cor. 13:12
[17] John Navone, *Toward a Theology of Beauty* (Collegeville, Minn.: Liturgical Press, 1996), vi.

Once the perfection of beauty, Zion shined forth God's presence.[18]

Now we listen to serpents—creations—instead of the Creator.[19]

> Therefore, the land mourns, and all who dwell in it languish, and also the beasts of the field and the birds of the heavens, and even the fish of the sea are taken away.[20]

Now, no matter where we are, it seems we perpetually sit by the waters of Babylon, exiled by empire and injustice and disorder.

We weep because exile desires us to lose the beautiful.

So, we hang up our instruments and fail to sing our songs.

> How shall we sing the LORD's song in a foreign land?[21]

Indeed, how shall we ever muster the energy to find the goodness to sing? How, in the hardest days of exile and the resultant pit of despair, can we find life and its beauty again?

Perhaps, in the midst of this present exile, beauty finds us through the subtle whispers of imagination. If we can cultivate

---

[18] See Ps. 50:2
[19] See Gen. 3
[20] Hosea 4:3
[21] Ps. 13:4

the courage to allow imagining and trust, God very well may breathe into us new life out of the old . . .

Beauty from the ashes.

As it says in the Scriptures:

> Thus says the Lord GOD: On the day that I cleanse you from all your iniquities, I will cause the cities to be inhabited, and the waste places shall be rebuilt.
>
> And the land that was desolate shall be tilled, instead of being the desolation that it was in the sight of all who passed by.
>
> And they will say, "This land that was desolate has become like the garden of Eden."[22]

It is the beauty of Isaiah's imagination and poetry amid exile that reminds us:

> "The wolf and the lamb shall graze together; the lion shall eat straw like the ox, and dust shall be the serpent's food. They shall not hurt or destroy in all my holy mountain," says the LORD.[23]

Maybe when Babylon's shadow looms larger and larger, we must remind ourselves that beauty can rescue us from the depths because it is our connecting point with God.

---

[22] Ezek. 36:33–35
[23] Isa. 65:25

When we choose courage, especially the boldness to create potential and newness, to create poetry and art, music, dance, liturgy, and . . . well, beauty amid the pain of exile, we are proclaiming (against all appearances) the greater reality that God is near.

It is beauty that awakens us, as it reveals that God is with us.

005 Beauty Is with Us

CHAPTER 005

Beauty Is with Us

The book of Exodus begins with a deep realization of the suffering that comes with life east of Eden. Enslaved and oppressed, the power of empire pushes harder and harder daily.

No celebration or worship or Sabbath—just more bricks and less straw.

And though they are creating great works of art, they are marked by abuse and oppression and coercion.

It is tainted beauty.

And so, God "looked down on the people of Israel and knew it was time to act."[24] And in mighty acts of power, God delivered the people on an exodus out of Egypt and into a new adventure, a new reality. Not one identified by slavery and oppression and

---

[24] Exod. 2:25

empire. No, this reality is identified by celebration, provision, memory, and Sabbath.

And the people respond with beauty.

The Scriptures state that:

> Then Moses and the people of Israel sang this song to the LORD, saying, "I will sing to the LORD, for He has triumphed gloriously; the horse and his rider He has thrown into the sea. The LORD is my strength and my song, and He has become my salvation; this is my God, and I will praise Him, my father's God, and I will exalt Him."[25]

Unfortunately, the celebration is short lived.

Why is it that when we reside on the brink of true freedom in our lives, there is always something sinister that lurks nearby and comes along at just the right moment to strip us of that hope?

For the children of Israel, this is one such moment. The draw of Egypt is strong, and the people begin turning their energies from worshiping the God of the Exodus to crafting idols for themselves. Safe gods fashioned out of gold: the idols of oppression and wealth and self. And though a work of art, it is—

Tainted beauty.

---

[25] Exod. 15:1–2

But Yahweh has a different, maybe even subversive, plan. He calls craftsmen to:

> Devise artistic designs, to work in gold and silver and bronze, in cutting stones for setting, and in carving wood, for work in every skilled craft. . ... He has filled them with skill to do every sort of work done by an engraver or by a designer or by an embroiderer in blue and purple and scarlet yarns and fine twined line, or by a weaver—by any sort of workman or skilled designer.[26]

God calls the people to craft a tent with aesthetics that would exemplify the beauty of Eden. Unlike the world's beauty, Eden was about glory, presence, harmony, *shalom*, and liberation.

There is a profound truth in this. This is the grander story of beauty that God offers. Unlike the tainted, seductive, oppressive "beauty" that the world offers—

Authentic beauty always liberates.

This tent would be the place that God's glory would fill. It was His beauty that reminded them that God was with them.

> Then the cloud covered the tent of meeting, and the glory of the LORD filled the tabernacle.[27]

Biblical scholar G.K. Beale writes that:

---

[26] Exod. 35:32, 33, 35
[27] Exod. 40:34

> In all of the OT that God's presence is spoken of as a cloud dwelling" is with respect to God's presence above the tabernacle. . ... Even the verb "to dwell" (*sa-kan*) could be rendered "to tabernacle."[28]

God dwelled with humanity! But it would not last. Over the generations, Israel hardened to the ways of God, the Temple was destroyed, and the glory departed. Exile became a visceral reality once again.

> Then the glory of the LORD went out from the threshold of the house. [29]

But the beauty of God's presence would not depart forever. The poetic prophet Isaiah courageously claimed within the struggle of occupation from foreign empires that:

> Therefore, the Lord Himself will give you a sign. Behold, the virgin shall conceive and bear a son, and shall call his name Immanuel.[30]

Immanuel means God is with us. The New Testament author Matthew takes it even further when he writes:

> Now the birth of Jesus Christ took place in this way. When his mother Mary had been betrothed to Joseph, before they came together she was found to be with child from the Holy Spirit. And her husband Joseph, being a just man and unwilling to put her to shame, resolved to divorce her quietly.

---

[28] G.K. Beale, *A New Testament Biblical Theology: The Unfolding of the Old Testament in the New* (Grand Rapids: Baker, 2011), 609.
[29] Ezek. 10:18a
[30] Isa. 7:14

> But as he considered these things, behold, an angel of the Lord appeared to him in a dream, saying, "Joseph, son of David, do not fear to take Mary as your wife, for that which is conceived in her is from the Holy Spirit.
>
> She will bear a son, and you shall call his name Jesus, for he will save his people from their sins."
>
> All this took place to fulfill what the Lord had spoken by the prophet: "Behold, the virgin shall conceive and bear a son, and they shall call his name Immanuel" (which means, God with us). When Joseph woke from sleep he did as the angel of the Lord commanded him: he took his wife, but knew her not until she had given birth to a son. And he called his name Jesus.[31]

Jesus, the preexisting Son and *Logos* (Word) of God, is born!

The Gospel of John puts it this way:

> And the Word became flesh and dwelt among us, and we have seen his glory, glory as of the only Son from the Father, full of grace and truth.[32]

The word "dwelt" brings us back to the image of the tabernacle. We could read this as "the Word became flesh and pitched His tent among us." God's glory has returned in the most unexpected of ways!

---

[31] Matt. 1:18–25
[32] John 1:14

His glory and splendor were not manifest through thunder and lightning nor through great acts of power or magnificent processions. Rather, God's glorious splendor has come to forever dwell with us, and it was inaugurated in—

The unassuming beauty of a newborn's face.

006 The Beautiful Savior

CHAPTER 006

The Beautiful Savior

Christ's life is the mark of beauty because in Jesus, we can peer into the face of the One who is truly beautiful.

Being the eternal *Logos*, the Word made flesh, He understood the art of speech, and He could craft stories that spoke into the heart and transformed lives. His very utterances would calm storms, liberate the oppressed, and bring sight.

We could point to Jesus' incarnation, His acts of healing, and His gentleness, as each of these are beautiful in their own way. Yet each act leads up to the time surrounding the preparation of His crucifixion . . . a most gruesome and pitiful experience that, in some deeply mysterious way, demonstrated a most profound beauty.

How is it that in many of our most meaningful experiences and narratives, beauty and suffering find themselves in the same stories?

Considering the cross, is it possible that suffering might have something to do with beauty?

Writer Timothy Danaher makes this point by stating:

> Suffering and beauty. Both are mysteries which go together. Both make us cry—a strange and interesting phenomenon. Both wound us . . . and leave us searching for answers.[33]

Think about the stories leading up to Jesus' crucifixion. What might they teach us about this peculiar paradox?

> Now about eight days after these sayings [Jesus] took with him Peter and John and James and went up on the mountain to pray. And as he was praying, the appearance of his face was altered, and his clothing became dazzling white. And behold, two men were talking with him, Moses and Elijah, who appeared in glory and spoke of his departure, which he was about to accomplish at Jerusalem.[34]

During the transfiguration, Jesus underwent a beatific transformation in preparation for His "departure." The interesting thing about the word, "departure," is that in Greek, it literally means:

Exodus.

---

[33] Timothy Danaher, "Suffering and Beauty," *Dominicana*, February 26, 2016, https://www.dominicanajournal.org/suffering-and-beauty/.
[34] Luke 9:28–31

Jesus is transformed into a vivid reflection of His divine beauty to prepare for His crucifixion, which serves as a new exodus.

Because authentic beauty is always liberating.

Or think about the story of the disciples walking through the magnificent grandeur of the second temple.

> And as he came out of the temple, one of his disciples said to him, "Look, Teacher, what wonderful stones and what wonderful buildings!"
>
> And Jesus said to him, "Do you see these great buildings? There will not be left here one stone upon another that will not be thrown down."[35]

Jesus likens this temple to Himself elsewhere in the Gospel of John, where it says:

> Jesus answered them, "Destroy this temple, and in three days I will raise it up." The Jews then said, "It has taken forty-six years to build this temple, and will you raise it up in three days?"
>
> But he was speaking about the temple of his body. When therefore he was raised from the dead, his disciples remembered that he had said this, and they believed the Scripture and the word that Jesus had spoken.[36]

---

[35] Mark 13.1–2
[36] John 2.19–22

Many of the aspects of beauty in the First Testament, the glory of God, the tabernacle, the temple, and the exodus are all found in the stories surrounding Jesus' death.

One story in preparation for His death illustrates in a profound way how beauty and suffering stand together, as artist Makoto Fujimura explains:

> In Mark 14, Mary of Bethany barges in and breaks open this jar of nard that she's been saving up all her life. And the disciples are furious at her because she is doing what a woman should only be allowed to do on her wedding day, which was to anoint her bridegroom.
>
> Everybody knew what the aroma signified. They are expecting Jesus to kick her out, and Jesus says . . .
>
> "No, you have no idea. You don't understand this night. She has done a beautiful thing to me."
>
> Mary is responding to this encounter with Jesus when Jesus intentionally came late. He was supposed to come and heal Lazarus, her brother, and he's dead. So, she's very upset with him, I can imagine. And Jesus' answer to Mary was his tears.
>
> "Jesus wept."
>
> When Jesus wept, it was just gratuitous, useless beauty.
>
> And so, all she could do was to think, 'What is the most valuable thing that I have to offer back to him?' So, she grabs this jar, runs in. She wasn't thinking about this drama that she would create probably. But

what she knew was that Jesus is going to suffer, so the only thing she can do is anoint him.

But what she has done is beautiful and enduring because its ephemeral, because it's useless, because it's a waste.[37]

One of the fundamental aspects of this story is that "with each moment of misery comes the opportunity for love and compassion."[38]

And so, Jesus endures the pain, the suffering, and the terror of the cross.

In talking about this suffering servant, Isaiah writes:

> Behold, my servant shall act wisely; he shall be high and lifted up and shall be exalted. As many were astonished at you—his appearance was so marred, beyond human semblance, and his form beyond that of the children of mankind . . .
>
> He had no form or majesty that we should look at him, and no beauty that we should desire him.
>
> He was despised and rejected by men; a man of sorrows, and acquainted with grief; and as one from whom men hide their faces he was despised, and we esteemed him not. . . . Surely he has borne our griefs and carried our sorrows; yet we esteemed him stricken, smitten by God, and afflicted.

---

[37] Makoto Fujimura, "Episode 6: Wonder," *For the Life of the World: Letters to the Exiles* (Grand Rapids: Acton Institute, 2015).
[38] http://www.aboundlessworld.com/the-beauty-of-suffering/

> But he was pierced for our transgressions; he was crushed for our iniquities; upon him was the chastisement that brought us peace, and with his wounds we are healed.[39]

Jesus, in His crucifixion, had no form that we would call beautiful, and yet through His life, we see something truly awe-inspiring.

His face contained a rare beauty, not because of its symmetry or fairness, but because of the look of self-sacrificing love.

We see that Jesus was and is the very essence of the beautiful. Maybe one of the most important things that Jesus' life shows us is that the beautiful consists not only in an earthy, reflected beauty or in aesthetic values.

Perhaps, beauty is also an event.

Scholar Bruno Forte explains this characteristic of beauty when he writes:

> Beauty is an event; beauty happens when the Whole offers itself in the fragment, and when this self-giving transcends infinite distance.[40]

The incarnation, childhood, ministry, healings, teachings, crucifixion, resurrection, ascension . . . all events of beauty.

---

[39] Isa. 52:13–14; 53:2c–5
[40] Bruno Forte, *The Portal of Beauty: Towards a Theology of Aesthetics* (Grand Rapids: Eerdmans, 2008), vii.

Therefore, it is through the event of the cross that beauty and suffering come together in such a jarring way that it shakes us, evokes us, and pains us to awaken to the real, the present, and the true.

Adam was placed in the temple of God's glory, Eden, a serene and beautiful garden, and through actions of self-seeking, ushered ugliness and disorder and sin into the creation experience.

Christ entered ugliness and disorder and sinfulness, a broken world gripped in the throes of heart-wrenching pain, and ushered in salvation, peace, and beauty.

As the apostle Paul writes concerning Jesus:

> Who, though he was in the form of God, did not count equality with God a thing to be grasped, but emptied himself, by taking the form of a servant, being born in the likeness of men.
>
> And being found in human form, he humbled himself by becoming obedient to the point of death, even death on a cross.
>
> Therefore, God has highly exalted him and bestowed on him the name that is above every name, so that at the name of Jesus every knee should bow, in heaven and on earth and under the earth, and every tongue confess that Jesus Christ is Lord, to the glory of God the Father.[41]

Jesus, who was the form of beauty Himself, exchanged source beauty (sacred, pure, divine) for reflected beauty (earthy,

---

[41] Phil. 2:6–11

tainted, fragmented) to reveal the fullness of God's glory and, through His death and resurrection, triumph over the powers of evil, division, exile, and disorder.

He overpowered tainted, seductive, destructive beauty.

Through this exchange of beauty and the work of Christ, God began to inaugurate His beautiful and just Kingdom on earth as in the heavens.

He is restoring the broken image.

He is renovating Eden.

And He is with us through it all.

> And behold, I am with you always, to the end of the age.[42]

He is with us, to create a new humanity, a new creation through His beautiful church.

---

[42] Matt. 28:20b

007 The Beautiful Church

CHAPTER 007

The Beautiful Church

Jesus, before His departure, started a community—a community whose purpose is to dedicate herself to Christ's call, to the Way, to a life of faith and . . . beauty?

Could it be that the community of God, the church, is called to find the beautiful, and that it is possible that her heart might just depend on it?

Scottish theologian P.T. Forsyth once observed:

> Faith without a sense of beauty, or a religion severed from imagination and "over-engrossment with public and practical affairs," leaves us with a drought in our own souls. It no longer evokes a sense of wonder.[43]

---

[43] As found in Thomas Troeger, "The Necessity of Beauty," *Reflections, Divine Radiance: Keeping Faith with Beauty* (New Haven: Yale Divinity School, 2015).

What if the church is meant to be a place of beauty? Not just its buildings or programs or music or art,[44] but what if beauty is central to our mission? And what if, somewhere along the way, we have missed this central truth of our faith?

In the ancient Greek, there is this interesting connection between *kalos* (good, beautiful) and *kalein* (to call or summon).

In addition to beauty, the church is also referenced in the New Testament as the *ekklesia*: the called-out ones.

Maybe beauty is meant to call us out of the world and into the splendid transcendence of God as we journey through our present exile.

Unfortunately, discipleship has largely unnoticed its need to participate in the mission of God's beauty through our faith communities.

As Fujimura again, states:

> The church has exiled beauty from its conversations. And I think that we need to rediscover the beautiful in order to recover ourselves, our humanity.
>
> Jesus seemed to indicate that beauty is a door into the Gospel.[45]

---

[44] It must be said that the artistic beauty of our meeting places is not insignificant. It is there that all people have access to beauty, rich and poor alike, unlike many places where exquisite art is reserved for those who have the wealth to pay for it. If beauty is our connecting point with God, this may be a significant point.

[45] Fujimura, "Episode 6."

Interestingly, the apostle Paul uses the image of beauty to discuss his own mission.

> But thanks be to God, who in Christ always leads us in triumphal procession, and through us spreads the fragrance of the knowledge of him everywhere.
>
> For we are the aroma of Christ to God among those who are being saved and among those who are perishing, to one a fragrance from death to death, to the other a fragrance from life to life.[47]

Paul leads us back to a relevant cultural example, whereby the Romans celebrated the victory of the Emperor in battle. Can you imagine the scene? There might have been a parade, a procession to celebrate the good that he had accomplished.

And there would be singing, songs that recounted the victories and celebrated the king's prowess. There would be dancing and fragrances abounding to declare the triumph.

And Paul uses this image to say that this is us: a community spreading the fragrance of Christ for the blossoming of the life of the world.

Elsewhere, Paul uses another word to describe the church: *poema*. And *poema* means—

Masterpiece. We, as the church, are God's masterpiece!

We are beautiful.

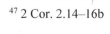[47] 2 Cor. 2.14–16b

When we embrace this identity as a community and respond with the beauty of worship to God's majesty and His triumph over the powers of hell and death and evil and disorder, we are joining in the royal procession and boldly proclaiming that there is one true King. We are cherishing that there are deeper truths than those the world offers us. And this is a stunning vision that Christ has given us.

However.

If we, as the church, lose this grasp of the beautiful, if we neglect to seek its place in our journey of faith, we might just lose sight of something significant, vital even.

So, how do we, as the church, embrace and keep this kind of beautiful?

There is another Greek word that comes up time and time again in Scripture that is the key to this. It is the word, *idou,* which means:

Behold.

As Fujimura states:

> Perhaps the greatest thing that we can do as a Christian community is to behold. Behold our God. Behold His creation. . ..
>
> God somehow demands of us so much more than just this transactional nature. It is really about the gift that we've been given, and the only response we can give back is with extravagance, with gratuitous beauty. And we need to tell this story. Not the story of pragmatism,

not the story of utility. This story of extravagance. Gratuitous beauty is the Gospel...

What really moves us tends to be someone who can behold.[48]

What if the church's mission—our worship, our outreach, our fight for justice, our work, and our identity—is both about beholding God's reflected beauty through creation and simply standing in wonder as we watch God in His eternal, Trinitarian dance?

But even more, what if, as the bride of Christ, we were meant to dance in eternal communion with Him as well?

And what if we see our evangelism as inviting people into the song and dance with us?

Maybe evangelism is less about persuasive techniques and well-formed apologetics...[49]

And more about joy, liberation, salvation, peace, community, and dancing.

One author puts it this way:

> So, the gospel comes to you not like a commercial on the radio or TV or a political slogan in a campaign or a scientific formula in a classroom, but like a song. It sneaks up on you, and then sneaks inside you.

---

[48] Fujimura, "Episode 6."
[49] Perhaps beauty is our greatest apologetic.

Somewhere in your journey through life, you begin to hear this song whose music captures your heart with its rhythm, melody, ambience, and glory, and you begin to move to its rhythm. Thus, you enter the dance.

Over time, your whole life begins to harmonize to the song. Its rhythm awakes you; its tempo moves you, so you resonate with its tone and flow with its melody. The lyric gradually convinces you that the entire world was meant to share in this song with its message, its joy, its dance.

If more people heard the music, their hatred would give way to reconciliation; their greed would melt into generosity; their grumbling would transform into gratitude; their mourning would be turned to dancing. . .. This is why if you begin to feel the song and live by it, you desire to help others do the same for a number of reasons . . . for the sheer beauty, truth, and goodness of the song.

Something this wonderful must be shared . . .for the good of your friends, neighbors, planet-mates who share the human predicament with you. As individuals, their lives would be enriched if they heard the song and learned to move with it . . . for the sake of the whole human race and the entire planet. If we humans don't learn to live by the beauty of the music, we'll live by our own destructive, greedy noise and despairing, consumptive silence, which will be disastrous for everyone and everything concerned . . . for the sake of the composer, the singer, the player—the Triune God whose song rings in every note and every beat with a spirit of sharing.

Anyone who hears the song—truly hears it—must dance. And all dancers seek to share their joy.[50]

So, we need a church who is unafraid to chart the choppy waters of God's wonder.

We need a church who can see into the beauty of creation, to see every person, regardless of nationality, race, age, and every creature, no matter how great or small, as a beautiful reflection of God's goodness.

We need a church who is unafraid to celebrate beauty, a beauty that is manifest from God's grandeur and resurrection, as well as displayed through God's actions on the cross.

We need a church who brings beauty back into the conversation, seeing beauty as a calling out from the world and entering into the door of the Gospel.

We need a church who will fill each space they enter with the captivating fragrance of God in unashamed brilliance.

We need a church who peers into the Triune God's joyous dancing and says, "Maybe we should dance too," and is courageous enough to join in.

And finally, we need a church who utilizes every aspect of their lives to invite others into this dance, who are courageous in creating newness during our present exile regardless if their work is in the office, in a restaurant, on a construction site, in

---

[50] Brian D. McLaren, *More Ready Than You Realize: Evangelism as Dance in the Postmodern Matrix* (Grand Rapids: Zondervan, 2002), 16–17.

a garage, in a factory, from a pulpit, in front of a canvas, at home with their children, or in a classroom.

We must see that these places provide the perfect environments needed for celebration, for joy . . .

For dancing.

Because it is in this dance that we learn to find the beautiful.

008 Finding Beautiful

CHAPTER 008

Finding Beautiful

What is beauty and where may it be found? This entire book has been a meditation, an endeavor into this uncharted territory we call the beautiful.

I do not make the case that this is the final word; rather, we have only grazed the surface of the proverbial iceberg in terms of the magnitude of beauty.

But in this last chapter, I now invite you to embrace the courage that it takes to find the beautiful. The charge is given, the foundation is set, and now may you set off on this seldom-mapped course, this path that leads to the One who is beauty.

In what follows, I make a series of summary observations on the nature, mystery, and wonder of beauty.

For as scholar Hans Urs Von Balthasar once wrote of the necessity of beauty:

Beauty is the word that shall be our first.

Beauty is the last thing which the thinking intellect dares to approach, since only it dances as an uncontained splendor around the double constellation of the true and the good and their inseparable relation to one another.

Beauty is the disinterested one without which the ancient world refused to understand itself . . . a world which both imperceptibly and yet unmistakably has bid farewell to our new world . . . a world of interests, leaving it to its own avarice and sadness.

No longer loved or fostered by religion, beauty is lifted from its face as a mask, and its absence exposes features on that face which threaten to become incomprehensible to man. We no longer dare to believe in beauty and we make of it a mere appearance in order the more easily to dispose of it.

Our situation today shows that beauty demands for itself at least as much courage and decision as do truth and goodness, and she will not allow herself to be separated and banned from her two sisters without taking them along with herself in an act of mysterious vengeance.

We can be sure that whoever sneers at her name as if she were an ornament of a bourgeois past—whether he admits it or not can no longer pray and soon will no longer be able to love.[51]

---

[51] Hans Urs Von Balthasar, *The Glory of the Lord: A Theological Aesthetics, Seeing the Form*, Volume 1 (San Francisco: Ignatius Press, 1982), 18.

Let us bravely reclaim beauty so that we may pray and love unhindered. Let us imagine beauty together.

Beauty is the very nature of being; it doesn't need a product, a page, an industry, or an affirmation from others.

Being, in its raw, unhindered self, is beautiful.

Beauty happens when chaos is ordered.

Humanity, in all its disorder and awkwardness, is beautiful. We are so beautiful in God's eyes, in fact, that Jesus came to die for us.

Beauty is the way that the light of the sun folds around your loved one.

Beauty is the brightness in the eyes of a child.

Beauty is in the orderly elegance of a song, whether the tinkering of a toddler or the skilled hands of a composer.

Beauty is in the artistic curvature of the lines that form through the experiences of the aged.

Beauty is when wounds of all kinds are healed.

Beauty is when suffering, in all its distortion and pain, brings about forgiveness, redemption, reconciliation, and compassion.

Beauty is when an addict (whether addicted to substances, images, fears, or self) finds deliverance because . . .

Authentic beauty always liberates.

Beauty is when something once broken is now restored.

Beauty is in the boldness of creating and imagining in the face of depression and exile.

Beauty is in the joy of birth . . . of a child, of a new path, of a new relationship, of a new believer.

Beauty is in the artist who pours themselves into their work . . . whatever that work may be.

Beauty is in integrity, proportion, and clarity.

Beauty is about order. Order is about proximity. Proximity is about relationship. And relationships are about justice.

Beauty is found in justice.

Beauty elevates us beyond the pedestrian.

Beauty is painful transcendence.

Beauty is in the saying, "Jesus wept."

Beauty is often thought of as the stuff of the earth, what we have defined as "reflected beauty."

But as the stuff of the earth reminds us, beauty is higher.

As ancient church leader Augustine once said:

What am I loving when I love you? Not bodily beauty nor the gracefulness of age; nor light's brightness, so dear to these eyes of mine; not the sweet melodies of song, nor the fragrance of flowers, of perfumes, of aromas; not manna, nor honey; not the body so dear to the embraces of the flesh: no, these are not the things I love when I love my God.

And yet in a certain sense I do love light and sound, smell and food and embrace, when I love my God, the light, sound, smell, food, and embrace of my inner being. There, a light shines for my soul untrammeled by space; there, I hear a sound that does not disappear into time; there, I smell a perfume that the wind does not carry off; there, I savor things that no gluttony makes sickly; there, I experience an embrace never to be broken by [excess]. All this I love when I love my God.

So, then I asked the earth, "What is all this?" and it replied: "It is not me." And all the things on earth gave me the same answer.

I quizzed the sea and its depths, the living things that move there, and they replied: "We are not your God, seek higher."

And then I said to all those things seated before the door of my senses, "If it is not you, tell me something about my God, speak to me of Him." And with a mighty voice all cried:

"He is our Creator." I looked at the creatures and asked; their beauty was their answer.[52]

---

[52] Augustine, "Book X," *Confessions* 6, 8.

Beauty is about the source of all being.

God is the source of the beautiful.

He is the Beauty beyond beauty.

God is the one who is transforming everything into something more glorious . . . something new. As is written in the book of Revelation:

> Then I saw a new heaven and a new earth, for the first heaven and the first earth had passed away, and the sea was no more. And I saw the holy city, new Jerusalem, coming down out of heaven from God, prepared as a bride adorned for her husband. And I heard a loud voice from the throne saying, "Behold, the dwelling place of God is with man. He will dwell with them, and they will be his people, and God himself will be with them as their God. He will wipe away every tear from their eyes, and death shall be no more, neither shall there be mourning, nor crying, nor pain anymore, for the former things have passed away." And he who was seated on the throne said, "Behold, I am making all things new."[53]

The writer goes on to use images of precious stones, weddings, the temple, and the garden of Eden to describe this new thing that is happening.

Eternally sitting at this table of celebration in the perfection of the new Eden with God in His resplendence as He graces the table with His presence is supremely beautiful.

---

[53] Rev. 21:1–5a

We began this exploration of beauty by asking questions such as, "What is beauty?" and, "Is beauty something held in the eye of the beholder?"

What we have seen is that beauty is so much more than something aesthetic or pleasing in a person's eyes. Rather—

Finding the beautiful is about joining the path of life with others and finding, at the end of that path, the One who is beauty, standing with arms wide open, eager to embrace His weary child.

May you realize that this endeavor into beauty has the capacity to lead you, me, all of us into something holy . . . something sublime.

Gregory of Nyssa once stated, "Concepts create idols; only wonder understands."

His insight gives us the path into understanding authentic beauty, for it is only when we are elevated beyond intellect, reason, and utility and find ourselves caught in the mystery of God's wonder that we can truly touch beauty.

And so, may you bring the fragrance of God's beauty everywhere you go.

May you realize that you are beautiful, something to behold, because you reflect the image of the One who is beauty.

You are His poem, His artwork, His . . .

Masterpiece.

May you embrace this identity as you seek out the darkest corners of our world. And as you find these forgotten places in the shadows of Babylon, may you seek to bring the beautiful in these places of deep need.

May you take on the call to bring the beauty of God into the ashes of a chaotic world. Because the world yearns for such bravery.

And finally, may you join the community of God in embracing and believing in the mystery and wonder of beauty.

For when we all are caught in such wonder that we can reach out and grasp the hem of Beauty's robe, we may just understand the truth that . . .

"Beauty will save the world."[54]

---

[54] Fyodor Dostoevsky, *The Idiot*, trans. Constance Garnett (New York: Bantam, 1981), 370.

Bibliography

Augustine, "Book X," *Confessions*. 6, 8.

Bancewicz, Ruth. "Beauty, Science, and Theology, Part 3," July 25, 2012. http://biologos.org/blogs/archive/beauty-science-and-theology-part-3.

Beale, G.K. *A New Testament Biblical Theology: The Unfolding of the Old Testament in the New*. Grand Rapids: Baker, 2011.

Danaher, Timothy. "Suffering and Beauty." *Dominicana*, February 26, 2016. https://www.dominicanajournal.org/suffering-and-beauty/.

Dostoevsky, Fyodor. *The Idiot*. Trans. Constance Garnett. New York: Bantam, 1981.

Feinberg, Margaret. *The Organic God*. Grand Rapids: Zondervan, 2007.

Forte, Bruno. *The Portal of Beauty: Towards a Theology of Aesthetics*. Grand Rapids: Eerdmans, 2008.

Fujimura, Makoto. "Episode 6: Wonder." *For the Life of the World: Letters to the Exiles*. Grand Rapids: Acton Institute, 2015.

http://www.aboundlessworld.com/the-beauty-of-suffering/

McLaren, Brian D. *More Ready Than You Realize: Evangelism as Dance in the Postmodern Matrix*. Grand Rapids: Zondervan, 2002.

Navone, John. *Toward a Theology of Beauty*. Collegeville, Minn.: Liturgical Press, 1996.

Piper, John. "How Pervasive and Practical is the Beauty of God?". July 7, 2013. www.desiringgod.org/articles/how-pervasive-and-practical-is-the-beauty-of-god.

Rybarczyk, Edmund J. *For Him Who Has Eyes to See: Beauty in the History of Theology*. Eugene, Ore.: Cascade, 2016.

Tripp, Paul. "Psalm 27: The Theology of Beauty." November 3, 2016. http://m.christianity.com/blogs/paul-tripp/psalm-27-the-theology-of-beauty.html.

Troeger, Thomas. "The Necessity of Beauty." *Reflections. Divine Radiance: Keeping Faith with Beauty*. New Haven: Yale Divinity School, 2015.

Von Balthasar, Hans Urs. *The Glory of the Lord: A Theological Aesthetics, Seeing the Form*, Volume 1. San Francisco: Ignatius Press, 1982.

ABOUT THE AUTHOR

Matthew S. Miller is a servant seeking the way of the King to build for His Kingdom and promote His glory. He is married to the love of his life, Linsey, and they have three beautifully rambunctious children. He holds a BS in wildlife and fisheries science from Tennessee Technological University, an MA in Christian Scripture from Heritage Christian University and is currently a PhD candidate in the Kearley Graduate School of Theology at Faulkner University. Matthew is the preaching, teaching, and discipleship minister at Highland Hills church of Christ in Tullahoma, Tennessee.

By Renewed Christian Living

Dear Sisters: Twelve Ways to Grow Authentic Community with Your Sisters in Christ
By Kaye Mayes

Movement: A 40-Day Spiritual Journey
By Matthew S. Miller

For us women, life can be a rush. Between working hard and taking care of our families, it is easy to lose connection with our sisters in Christ. And yet, these sisterly bonds provide the fertile soil needed for depth and growth in our life of faith. How can we maintain our everyday responsibilities while strengthening these connections? In *Dear Sisters,* Kaye Mayes develops twelve biblical principles that lead to authenticity in your interactions with other women as well as growth for your community of sisters. Kaye writes: "We are indeed sisters as God has adopted us into His family of believers and we are all siblings, not to be in rivalry, but to work together for the good of our Father to do His will. Who is our sister? Any woman who is also a child of God; an heir of righteousness through His Son, our Lord and Savior, Jesus Christ. As my sister, I would love to get to know you." This book is a conversation meant to stir sisters in Christ to greater faithfulness to God and one another. If you apply these twelve principles to your weekly journey, you will find deeper community and greater love as you grow into what it means to be a Dear Sister.

Life is busy. But the everyday rush shouldn't keep us from a deep, moving spirituality. In *Movement*, Matthew Miller invites you on a forty-day devotional journey toward intentional discipleship amid a culture that never stops. Each day provides busy adults with the opportunity to explore new depths of faith and compassionate change.

The devotions in this book will inspire and equip you to rediscover your passion for Christ as you endeavor on your own personal revolution. Through four stages (called movements), you will experience inward transformation and renewal as you join in the adventure of God's purpose for your life.

Books available now on Amazon!

Made in the USA
Monee, IL
29 August 2021